CHAD LAWSON

PIANO SHEET MUSIC COLLECTION

ISBN 978-1-70514-343-8

Visit Hal Leonard Online at
www.halleonard.com

Contact Us:
Hal Leonard
7777 West Bluemound Road
Milwaukee, WI 53213
Email: info@halleonard.com

In Europe, contact:
Hal Leonard Europe Limited
42 Wigmore Street
Marylebone, London, W1U 2RN
Email: info@halleonardeurope.com

In Australia, contact:
Hal Leonard Australia Pty. Ltd.
4 Lentara Court
Cheltenham, Victoria, 3192 Australia
Email: info@halleonard.com.au

Chad's Notes on the Songs

The Broad Sun – *The Broad Sun*

The Broad Sun (2017) and its follow-up, *The Waning Moon* (2018), were meant as a planetary theme. I'm enamored with stargazing and wanted to write a series of how I thought each planet's personality would sound. My hope is to return to the series as I'm beyond curious what the other planets have to say.

I Wish I Knew – *The Space Between*

When I was in my early teens, I wanted to quit piano (as many early teens do) and begged my parents to let me play guitar. Fortunately, though I couldn't see it at the time, they saw the potential I had at the 88s and simply said, "No." Little did I know what was to come with just a bit of practice, patience, and most importantly, perseverance. If only life were always so clear and direct with each step taken.

I Wrote You a Song – *You Finally Knew*

I once read if a person is mentioned in poetry or music or in a painting, they'll long live past their time on earth. Vincent Van Gogh, Emily Dickinson, Ella Fitzgerald—the list is endless—will all continue to live generation after generation as their legacy has been cemented in a painting, a poem, a song, etc. In 2020, my father passed. And while I'm no longer able to see or speak with him, I wanted his story to be shared with others long past even my life, touching the lives of listeners for decades to come. Though many will never know the intimate details behind "I Wrote You a Song," I'm certain they will feel the emotion within the piece and feel an embrace of something subtle, comforting and heartfelt, because that's exactly what my dad will forever be.

Islands – *Dark Conclusions: The Lore Variations*

All of the pieces from my *Lore Variations* were written for the podcast, "Lore." I consider Aaron Mahnke to be one of my very best friends, and when we decided to work together, he was completely hands-off. "Write whatever you're hearing," he said. When I write for "Lore," I don't score to the episode, as a composer would for film or television. I simply ask him, "What's one word that this episode is about?" And once he lets me know that word, whatever it may be, I then write what I feel the story would embrace. "Islands" was one of the first songs I wrote for the podcast and it's the opening song for every performance of "Lore" we do live. It's the perfect opener. I just love playing it.

Nocturne in A Minor – *The Piano*

This piece was written when a piano student "no-showed" for a lesson. I'm not kidding. I said to myself, "If Philip Glass had a no-show, and only an hour to write something, what would he write?" And while I consider myself nowhere near the brilliance of Glass, it was fun to wonder what he would do, had it been him. This has become my most recognized piece to date, which goes to show there's no such thing as the *perfect* time to create, but there's always a perfect time to *create* an opportunity.

Nocturne in F Minor, Op. 55, No.1 – *The Chopin Variations*

If Chopin were to write an album today, what would it sound like? There are so many people that have *heard* of Chopin but have never taken the time to listen to him. With *The Chopin Variations*, I decided to re-arrange some of his most known pieces and present them in a minimalist/ambient landscape.

Prelude in D Major – *You Finally Knew*

Melody. Everything, to me at least, is about the melody. I have a different approach when it comes to writing, in that I wait for the pieces to come to me in my mind. If I can't sing the piece while walking or doing an errand, it's not a piece I want to pursue. And when it is time to sit with pencil and paper, I always write the melody down first and *then* craft the chords and structure around the melody. Melody is everything, and this piece is a perfect example how once a melody is in place, the song simply writes itself.

St. John Passion (Johannespassion), *Christus der uns selig macht, BWV 245 – Bach Interpreted*

The *Chopin Variations* were such a success. So many people were saying, "I've never listened to Chopin and now I can't stop!" So, I decided to introduce my second favorite composer, J.S. Bach. Part of my daily practice is taking at least one Bach Chorale and playing through the piece to hear/learn the harmony, structure, melodies, etc. It's a tremendous tool in learning composition. With *Bach Interpreted*, I analyzed each chorale as if it were a jazz chart and found such beauty and awe in Bach's pieces. And, such a prolific composer and storyteller!

Stay – *You Finally Knew*

"Stay" is an invitation for the listener to find a tiny pocket of the day that's completely theirs. A few minutes reading a book, perhaps being overly detailed in making the perfect pour-over, or just sharing some time with a friend while walking outside; creating that place that rejuvenates you, encourages you, ignites you. That place you wish you could just "Stay."

Swan Lake – *The Piano*

I've always wanted to write a piece for ballet. And while this piece wasn't written for anything specifically, I've always thought it would be where I would "pick up from" once the opportunity presents itself.

The Waning Moon – *The Waning Moon*

See the notes for "The Broad Sun."

When the Party's Over

I love a great song, no matter the genre. A great song is a great song. And it just so happens that everything Finneas O'Connell and Billie Eilish create is usually that: a great song. Harmonically and analytically, the structure of "When the Party's Over" is so unique. Along with Eilish's deeply vulnerable vocal, I couldn't help but be drawn to this piece. It's the perfect combination of heart (Billie's vocals) and mind (Finneas's song structure). And when a song is so well crafted, it can stand on its own no matter the instrument playing it.

THE BROAD SUN

Written by CHAD LAWSON

Moderately, melancholy

With pedal

I WISH I KNEW

Written by CHAD LAWSON

Introspective (♩ = c. 60–63)

With generous pedal throughout

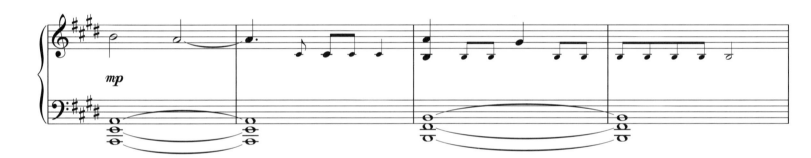

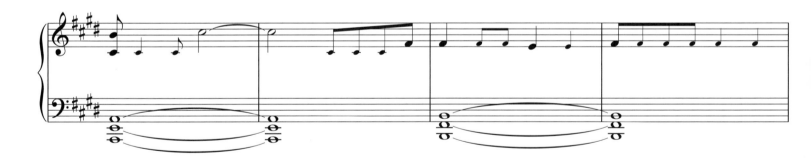

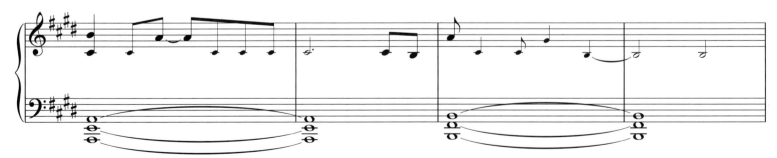

* *Small notes* **pppp** *throughout*

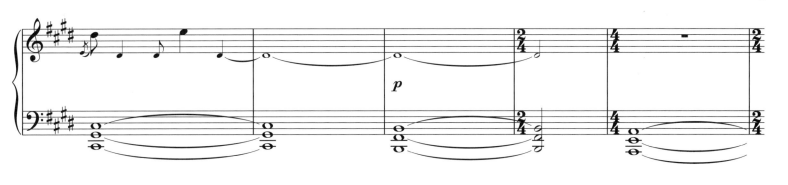

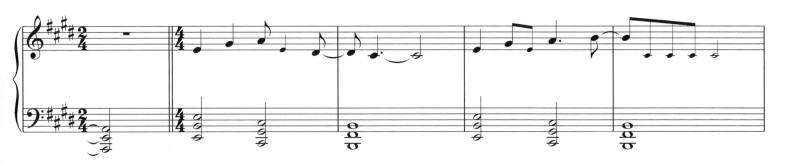

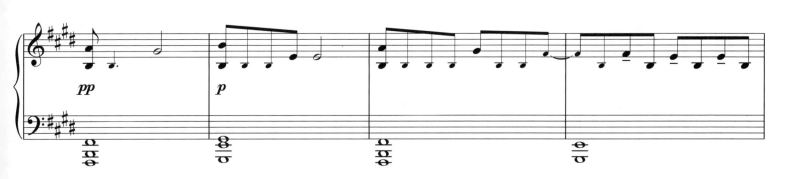

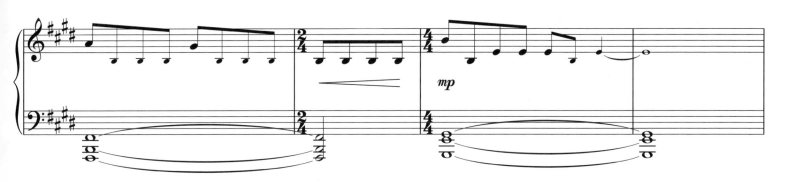

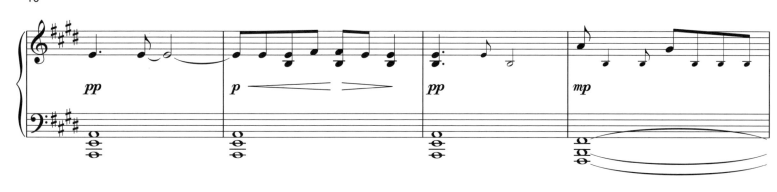

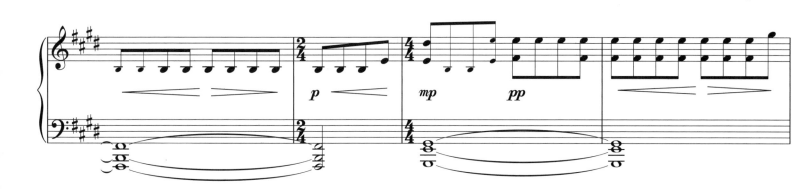

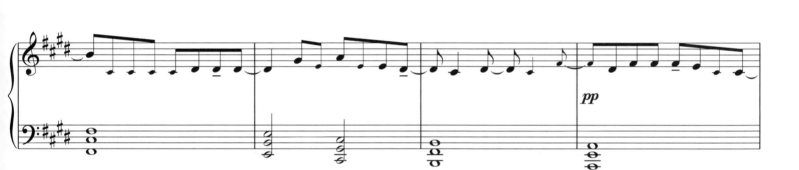

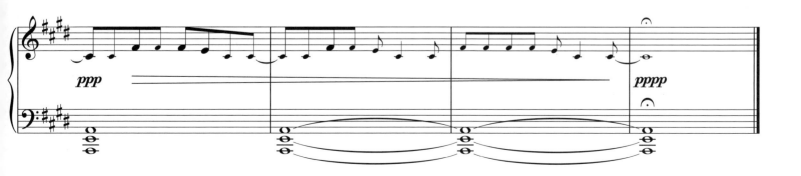

I WROTE YOU A SONG

Written by CHAD LAWSON

ISLANDS

Written by CHAD LAWSON

NOCTURNE IN A MINOR

Written by CHAD LAWSON

Faster, as before (♩. = c. 66)

NOCTURNE IN F MINOR
Op. 55, No. 1

Written by FREDERIC CHOPIN
Arranged by CHAD LAWSON

Andante (♩ = 72)

mp *sempre molto legato*

With pedal

Tempo I

PRELUDE IN D MAJOR

Written by CHAD LAWSON

THE WANING MOON

Written by CHAD LAWSON

ST. JOHN PASSION

(Johannespassion)
Christus, der uns selig macht, BWV 245

Written by JOHANN SEBASTIAN BACH
Arranged by CHAD LAWSON

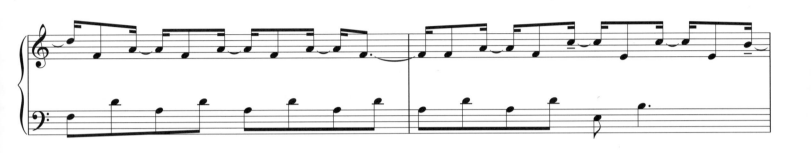

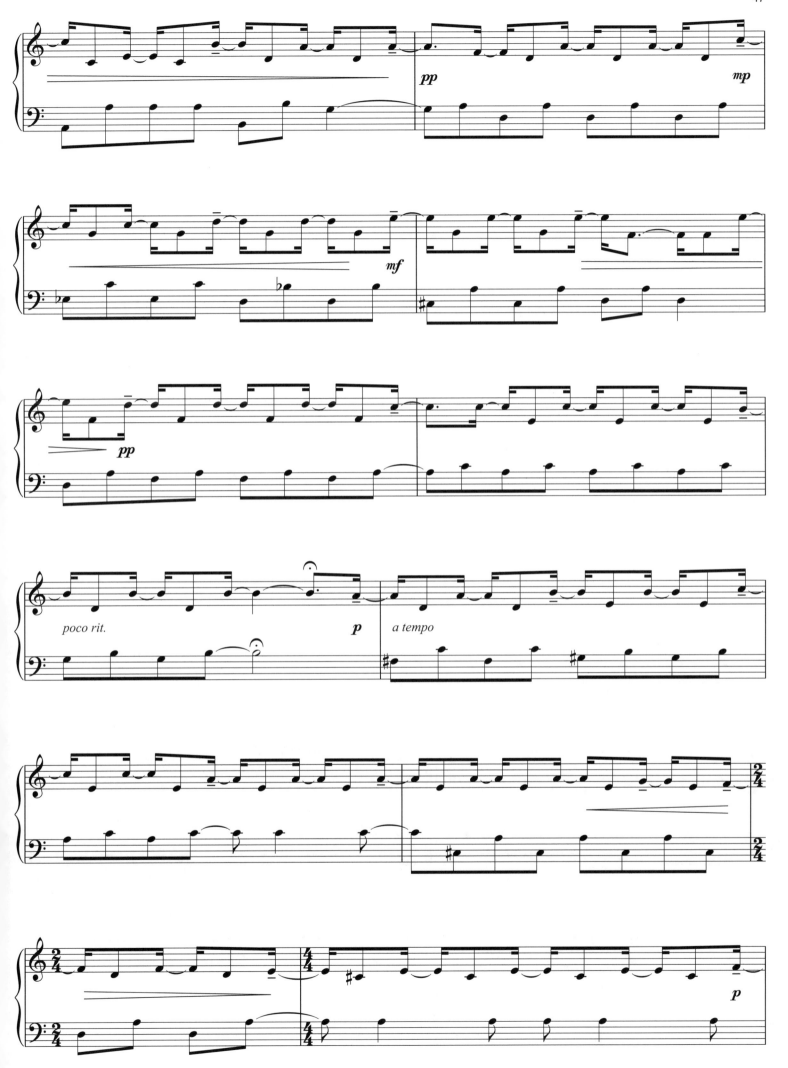

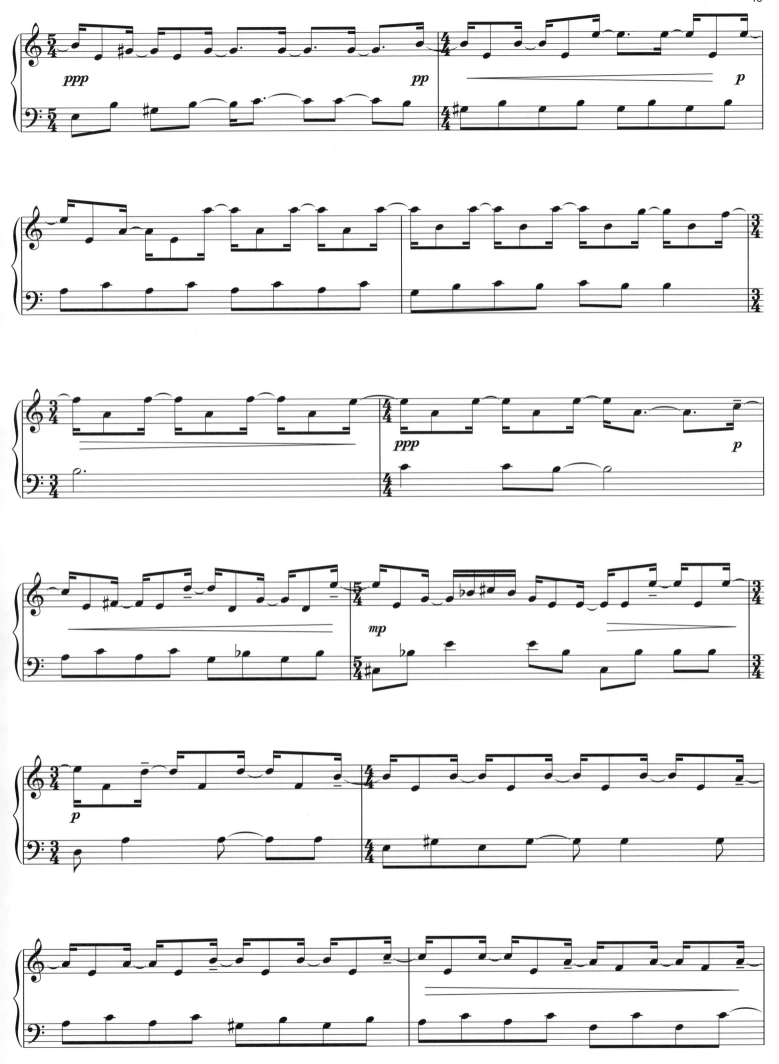

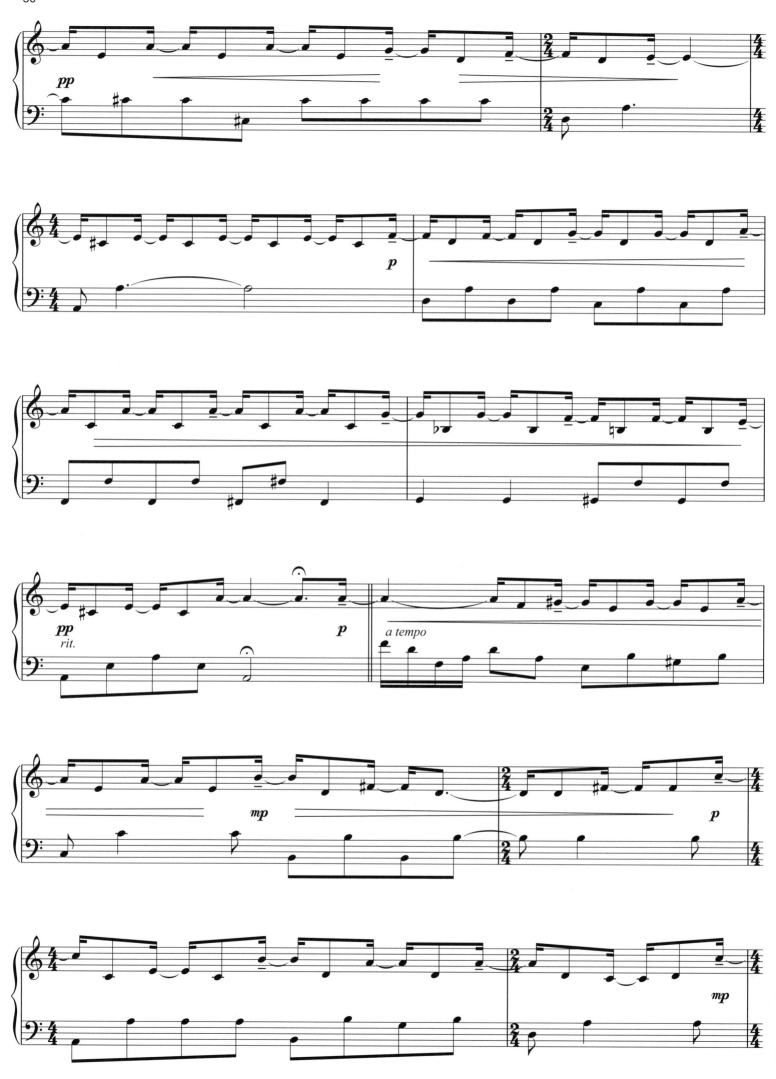

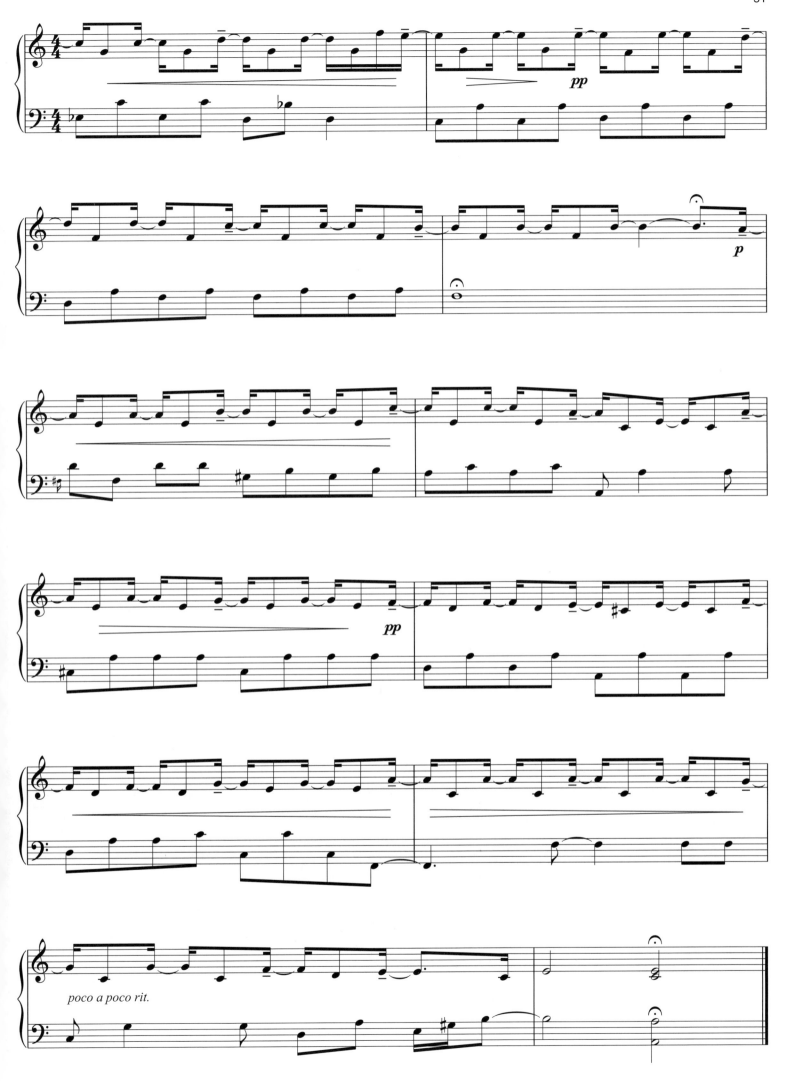

poco a poco rit.

STAY

Written by CHAD LAWSON

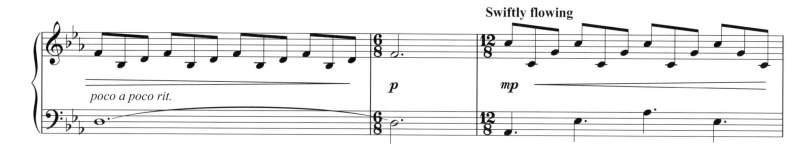

SWAN LAKE

Written by CHAD LAWSON

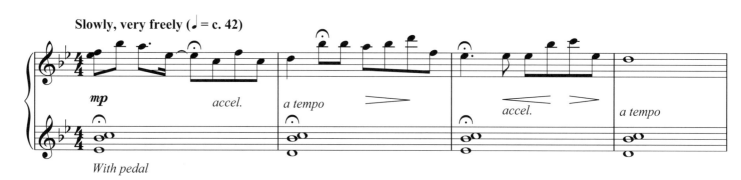

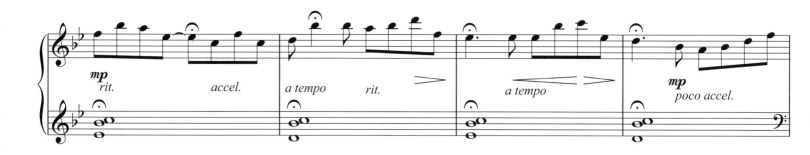

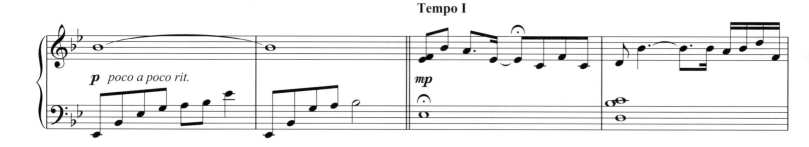

Faster, still freely (♩ = c. 60)

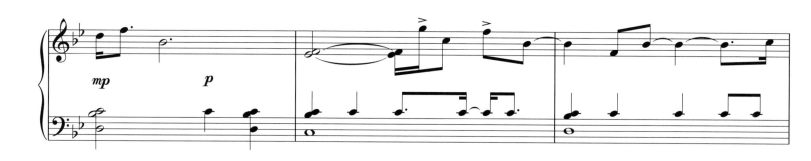

WHEN THE PARTY'S OVER

Words and Music by
FINNEAS O'CONNELL
Arranged by Chad Lawson